How To Survive Without Money

Downsizing and Living Without Money in Today's Economy

Dr. Leland Benton

TABLE OF CONTENTS

DISCLAIMER AND TERMS OF USE AGREEMENT 3
Introduction – To Gain is To Lose; To Lose is To Gain 5
Chapter 1 – To Live Big You Must First Become Small 9
Chapter 2 – Opportunity #1: Book Writing & Publishing 14
Chapter 3 – Opportunity #2: Ghostwriting 19
Chapter 4 - Opportunity #3: Amateur Internet Sleuth 25
Chapter 5 – Opportunity #4: Survival Planning 31
Chapter 6 – Opportunity #5: Internet Marketing 35
Chapter 7 – Opportunity #6: Miscellaneous Opportunities 44
Chapter 8 – Summary & Conclusions 53
I Have a Special Gift for My Readers 55
Meet the Author 56

How To Survive Without Money
Downsizing and Living Without Money in Today's Economy
©Copyright 2013 by Dr. Leland Benton

DISCLAIMER AND TERMS OF USE AGREEMENT:

(Please Read This Before Using This Book)

This information is for educational and informational purposes only. The content is not intended to be a substitute for any professional advice, diagnosis, or treatment.

The author and publisher of this book and the accompanying materials have used their best efforts in preparing this book.

The author and publisher make no representation or warranties with respect to the accuracy, applicability, fitness, or completeness of the contents of this book. The information contained in this book is strictly for educational purposes. Therefore, if you wish to apply ideas contained in this book, you are taking full responsibility for your actions.

The author and publisher disclaim any warranties (express or implied), merchantability, or fitness for any particular purpose. The author and publisher shall in no event be held liable to any party for any direct, indirect, punitive, special, incidental or other consequential damages arising directly or indirectly from any use of this material, which is provided "as is", and without warranties. As always, the advice of a competent legal, tax, accounting, medical or other professional should be sought where applicable.

The author and publisher do not warrant the performance, effectiveness or applicability of any sites listed or linked to in this book. All links are for information purposes only and are not warranted for content, accuracy or any other implied or explicit purpose. No part of this may be copied, or changed in any format, or used in any way other than what is outlined within this course under any circumstances. Violators will be prosecuted.

This book is © Copyrighted by ePubWealth.com.

Introduction – To Gain is To Lose; To Lose is To Gain

I am often asked, "Can you really survive in today's world without money?" Short answer – YES! I am not saying that you can survive COMPLETELY without money; even though I know quite a few people conducting a "barter economy" and doing quite well at it. One of the things to consider is where you live. It is more difficult to live without money in a large city rather than a small community like I live in here in Southern, Utah and it is much easier to live in a 'barter economy" in a small community too.

What I am saying is that you can easily cover the essentials – rent, power, food, etc easily by following what I teach here and by doing so; you can also release the financial stress and anxiety that the current economic downturn has brought to many families across the nation.

Beginning in 2008, everything went to hell in a hand basket. The real estate market crashed wiping out billions of dollars of equity. This very same equity was what a good many senior citizens were relying on to retire. With it gone, many seniors were left with a double whammy – their age prevented them from finding good jobs and they simply didn't have the money to retire.

In the book, "How To Retire Without Money," my associate, Dr. Noah Pranksky demonstrates just how easy it is to exist comfortably without money. This book shot to bestseller status in just three days of being released and published.

How To Retire Without Money
http://www.amazon.com/dp/B00B5R2ORE

Furthermore, in the book, "Getting Paid For Everything You Do," demonstrates how people can easily earn money online doing a variety of tasks that are easy and fun. This book also shot to bestseller status within a week of being released and published.

Getting Paid For EVERYTHING You Do!
http://www.amazon.com/dp/B00B03C0EA

When I read the reviews of both of the books cited above, I was stunned by the reader's responses to the many ways people could get by if they just followed the bouncing ball and put into practice what both books were teaching.

I was the adviser to both of the books cited above so when I saw that this topic was one of tremendous interest to people, I decide to write this book and pull it all together for my readers. The two books cited above work in conjunction with this book so I strongly urge you to buy them for your personal library.

No one is immune to what I will be teaching in this book including me. In Chapter 1, "To Live Big You Must First Become Small" I am going to show you how I became small and the benefits I obtained by doing so.

But then something really nice occurred. I was free from the responsibility of "STUFF" and it was actually exhilarating. I no longer had all this stuff to worry about, insure against loss or theft, keep clean, keep maintained, and more. The feeling had become so great I began looking around for what I could get rid of and I was amazed at all of the "stuff" I had accumulated and never used. In fact, the word 'amazed' just doesn't cut it here. I was actually left dumbfounded on what was before me that just sat there as useless assets. And when I woke up and realized that in many cases I was still paying to store it, insure it, maintain it, etc, I really became upset.

So in Chapter 1, I will begin the lesson by demonstrating how I did it and then I will move on to even meatier stuff that will enable you to live comfortably without the money you have been currently spending.

Now I need to put in a disclaimer here: I am a widower, my kids are grown and gone and I also make a very healthy income, which translates into a large monthly disposable income. Now I know most of my readers are not in my position so I am going to show you how I did it as if I was not in my current economic state.

Before I lost my wife, she was a very frugal woman. It didn't matter how much money I made, she operated as if we were penniless. She kept very detailed records, cut every blinking coupon out of the papers, and watched the cashiers as they rang up her purchases. She would fix things around the house rather than hire someone to fix it (I am very non-mechanical) and candidly there were times she drove me nuts with her penny pinching routine but there just was no way to convince her otherwise. I am convinced this was part of her DNA.

Everything I teach you in this book revolves around mindset. As a behavioral scientist, I know about mindset. This is not a get-rich-quick book and if your mindset believes that this is what you purchased then you need to close this book out and return it for a full refund. I only want serious people that have a strong desire to improve their personal financial condition and learn how to survive in today's world of economic uncertainty.

First I will teach you the benefits of downsizing but then in the meatier stuff I am going to introduce you to the concept of "passive income" where you can make money 24/7, even while you sleep and once you follow my instructions, the program takes over from there with no further involvement on your part. You are going to love this part of the instruction.

Today I am debt free, downsized and lean and mean. I have no financial worries and literally can do anything I want to do. Yes, my situation is different than yours but if I can do it then you can too. I am so confident that I can teach you how to duplicate what I have done that I am giving you my personal email address to write to me if you run into a problem or don't understand something. I will respond personally to all emails sent to me: lee.benton@epubwaealth.com.

So, let's begin with the lesson, "To Live Big You Must First Become Small" and then we will move on to the good stuff!

Chapter 1 – To Live Big You Must First Become Small

Small is the new BIG! And it is true! We live in a society of consumerism and entertainment and this way of living has literally exacerbated the economic downturn that began in 2008.

I want to define what I mean by Small is the New Big. Companies began downsizing to stay alive and weather the recession and you need to do the same by first examining all of the "stuff" you own and then making a plan to get rid of the stuff you don't use or need. Becoming "lean and mean" is what I am talking about here.

When I moved to Utah years ago, I had a mover give me a bid to move me. The bid was astronomical until I realized it would take 4-big moving vans to move me. AND I AM BY MYSELF FOR GOODNESS SAKES!!! I had accumulated so much stuff and even had four large storage units jammed full to the ceilings with more stuff. Ridiculous! Think about it for just a moment. I was paying exorbitant storage fees for storing stuff I didn't use. Talk about utter stupidity.

For years, my daughter had been suggesting I have a garage sale to get rid of all of it but I was too lazy and didn't want to be bothered. Meanwhile month after month I was paying to store things that I never even used.

I decided to have a serious look at everything. I admit; the bid from the mover is what caused this to happen. After some serious introspection, I called my daughters and told them to go to the storage units and take what they wanted because I was going to get rid of all of it.

They came running and told me to sit back because they would handle everything, which they did and did an excellent job I might add of disposing of all of the "stuff" I had accumulated over the years. As I witnessed the people going through all of the stuff I was literally stunned at what was in those four storage units. I had forgotten about most of the stuff in there. My daughters had removed all of the mementoes and personal stuff and all that was left were the things people would want. I even had a new washer and dryer in one of the storage units and I had no idea how they had gotten there. Weird!

Before the sale occurred, I went through my house and got rid of even more stuff I didn't use from clothes to furniture to tools…nothing was immune from my critical eye. And as I said previously, the feeling was exhilarating.

The mover returned to give me another bid and it went from four moving vans to one van. And the bid did not look like my social security number too!!!

After my move to Utah and once I got settled, I began scrutinizing all of my expenses and personal budget. Once again, I was shocked at what I discovered. Like most people, I had a mortgage, I had two car loans – one for my car and one for my truck – I also had credit card bills, insurance – property and casualty as well as health and life insurance – my food bill was astronomical since I ate out a lot, and last, the realization that I had become a catalog junkie and home shopping network junkie was rammed home when I saw just how many purchases I made online from catalogs and websites.

The results of looking at my personal finances caused me to make severe changes in my spending habits. I decided to make it my goal to become debt free. I outlined a plan to pay off my mortgage, my two car loans, my credit card debt, and reappraised all of my insurance and investments using the services of my bank's financial planner. I completely gave up my catalog purchases and online purchases and even started eating at home more rather than eating out.

Now, accomplishing this did not happen overnight and in fact, it took a little over two years to become debt free but today I have virtually no debt and everything I own is paid for. Everybody's situation is different but taking the frist step is important. Armed with a goal and the desire to relieve yourself of financial anxiety and stress is worth the effort in and of itself.

One of the things that came out of all of my downsizing efforts was the fact that my disposable income increased dramatically and my savings and investments increased too. I was now able to do anything I wanted to do because I was rid of everything that had been holding me back.

Next, I had completely revamped the asset and debt side of my balance sheet so I then turned my attention to the income producing side of my balance sheet. Again I was stunned at what I found.

Allow me to explain because this is what I called earlier "the meatier stuff".

I run 12-divisions of my company:

http://appliedmindsciences.com/
http://appliedwebinfo.com/
http://BookbuilderPLUS.com
http://embarrassingproblemsfix.com/
http://www.epubwealth.com/
http://forensicsnation.com/
http://neternatives.com/
http://privacynations.com/
http://survivalnations.com/
http://thebentonkitchen.com
http://theolegions.org

I make a healthy income but without realizing it, I had built a company centered on my passions.

I have been a behavioral scientist now for 32-years and hence my Applied Mind Sciences research facility was a big profit center.

Furthermore, I have also been a writer and author also for 32-years and hence my ePubWealth unit, which is a full service publishing house with over 1,000 authors under contract and with 40,000 plus book titles in our inventory and where I am Editor-in-Chief and my BookbuilderPLUS unit, both of which contribute heavily to my bottom line.

Another one of my passions is forensics science and hence, my ForensicsNation unit, which is one of my largest divisions where we identify, track and arrest cyber-criminals of all kinds and turn them into law enforcement.

Next, my PrivacyNations unit, which is all about privacy issues and my SurvivalNations unit, which is all about surviving a disaster/crisis both contribute heavily to my bottom line.

Last, my Neternatives internet marketing company and my cooking and baking website The Benton Kitchens also contribute to my bottom line and are two units I have fun with too.

The keyword and the most operative word here is "passion". I am convinced that these units have done well because they are all passions of mine and where I do not consider them "work".

Okay, here is my point: I am going to describe in the following chapters the various ways that you can make money working from home and employing your own passions.

You can do this as supplementary income to your existing career or full time; the choice is yours. Do not forget to downsize and I would recommend you do this first.

Now the book I mentioned earlier, "How To Get Paid For Everything You Do" describes what I will call the "everyday stuff" you can do to earn money working from home.

Getting Paid For EVERYTHING You Do!
http://www.amazon.com/dp/B00B03C0EA

What I want to do in the following chapters is describe opportunities for you that should be considered as "career stuff" or things you can do from home that can turn into big moneymaking units just like the ones of mine that I described above.

Most of all I will now introduce you to "passive income" and this is where you really need to pay attention.

Okay, let's get at it….

Chapter 2 – Opportunity #1: Book Writing & Publishing

To begin, I want to first introduce you to two very special words – PASSIVE INCOME!! Passive income is income you earn 24/7, day-after-day, month-after-month, even while you sleep where you first set it up and then there is no further involvement on your part; it is income that continues to pour in.

Writing books – authorship – and publishing books is one of the most lucrative passive income opportunities on the planet.

There are literally almost a hundred main publishing platforms available to self-publishing indie authors. But out of these hundred, there are six major publishing platforms where you can publish your books and in turn they will put them up on the various platforms listed. Here they are;

Kindle Direct Publishing – Owned by Amazon, this is the largest self-publishing platform on the net today. Amazon also owns CreateSpace: http://kdp.amazon.com/

Createspace - Standard: Amazon.com, Amazon Europe, Createspace Store. Expanded: Bookstores and Online Retailers, Libraries and Academic Institutions, Createspace Direct independent bookstores and book resellers: https://www.createspace.com/

Smashwords - Apple iBookstore, Barnes & Noble, Sony, Kobo, Diesel, Baker & Taylor: http://www.smashwords.com/

Lulu.com - Amazon .com US, UK, France, Germany, Italy, and Spain stores, $75 Ingram Catalog retailers Amazon.com, BN.com, local bookstores, etc, iBookstore: http://www.lulu.com

BookBaby - iBookstore, Amazon Kindle, Barnes and Noble PubIt, Sony eReader Store, Kobo, Copia, Gardner Books, Baker & Taylor Bookstore, eBook Pie, eSentral:
http://www.bookbaby.com/

BookLocker - Amazon.com, BarnesandNoble.com PubIt, BooksaMillion.com and many other smaller, online bookstores, both domestic and foreign. Any bookstore with an Ingram account can pick up Ingram's feed.
http://publishing.booklocker.com/

Now many of you may not be able to write a sentence but this doesn't matter. In my best-selling book, "How To Write a Kindle Book in Hours," I explain the different ways that you can write books without having the talent of being a writer yourself.

How to Write a Kindle Book in Hours
http://www.amazon.com/dp/B008XOY8VC

I offer free webinars that teach people everything they need to know about the self-publishing business. Go here and download the free webinar recordings as well as all the goodies I give away.

Webinar Download Portals
http://tinyurl.com/epubwebinar
http://tinyurl.com/epubwebinar2
http://tinyurl.com/epubwebinar3

I also offer an advanced class for people who require one-on-one instruction. Go here for more details:

http://www.epubwealth.com/epubwealth-advanced-program/

Everything I teach is part of my ePublishing series of book:

Copyright Law Guidebook – Learning the ins-outs of copyright law is easy with this guidebook. It contains everything that authors should be aware of and incorporate into their manuscripts.
http://www.amazon.com/dpB00BHEYBK8

How to Promote Your Book Online & Offline – writing a book is part of it; advertising, marketing and promotion is the other part. Learn how to pulse your book to best-selling status with this book.
http://www.amazon.com/dp/B00AS7PDCK

How To Promote Your Book Online & Offline Vol 2 – More book promotion and marketing techniques to assist in your book sales.
http://www.amazon.com/dp/B00BDTEILO

How to Write a Kindle Book in Hours – Don't be left out of the self-publishing indie author craze. Even if you cannot write a single word, this book will show you how to cash in on book publishing
http://www.amazon.com/dp/B008XOY8VC

How to Write Compelling Content – Content is king and keeps your readers coming back for more. Learn how to write compelling content with this book.
http://www.amazon.com/dp/B00B5QWYTI

International Standard Book Numbers – ISBNs are important and are required by all of the publishing platforms. Learn all about ISBNs in this book and learn to do it right the first time.
http://www.amazon.com/dp/B00B2YB4SK

Promoting Your Video Book Trailers – Promoting your books on YouTube and the hundreds of free video sharing site increases your book sales exponentially. This book teaches you how to do videos as well as provides subcontractors to do it for you.
http://www.amazon.com/dp/B00BCDHEMG

Publish with a Purpose – Ghostwriting can be super profitable. Learn how to become a ghostwriter and how to write books for

business owners at the same time. Once you purchase this book, the download portal will also provide you with a sample video book trailer and sample legal agreement to use to contract your services with clients.
http://www.amazon.com/dp/B008Z5U4LC

The ePubWealth Program – this is the basic authoring course which describes how to write books and the publishing platforms that sell them for you.
http://www.amazon.com/dp/B008HHHVO6

The ePubWealth Program ADVANCED – This is one of the most advanced book writing and marketing courses on the net today with over $10,000 in downloads available once you sign up.
http://www.amazon.com/dp/B00B65PGCA

The Publishing Agreement – if you use a publishing house to publish your books then you need to know about publishing agreements.
http://www.amazon.com/dp/B00BKGTQZ

Currently I personally have over 200-books published on the Amazon Kindle platform alone and it isn't even my most profitable platform. Smashwords is my most profitable platform, then Lulu.com and third is Amazon kindle. On all three platforms I am making a healthy five figure monthly income from each platform…do the math. On Kindle I make a 70% royalty on all my books sold; book writing and publishing is lucrative.

Can you do this? Yes, you can and with my one-on-one instruction, I can get you to best-selling author status quickly. Like I said, even if you cannot string words together to form a single sentence, I can show you how to cash in on book publishing.

Without a doubt this is one of the best if not "THE" best forms of passive income. Please consider this opportunity carefully.

Authors are important. Without authors the world would be ignorant. We entertain, we cajole, we teach and we make a difference. The world still holds authors in high esteem and rightly so because authors change the way we think, the way we live and the way we live our lives. My email inbox is stuffed daily from readers and their success stories and I engage my readers because they are important to me. Without my readers, my words fall to the ground and mean nothing.

Becoming an author means that you are making a difference in other people's lives. My passions translate into more than just income. The results of my work are evident from the emails I receive from my readers. I wouldn't give up being an author if you put a gun to my head. It is without a doubt the most rewarding of my career paths.

Authorship involves so many avenues of opportunities I literally cannot list them all here but my books on ePublishing above speaks about most of them. I will touch on one that is very lucrative…Ghostwriting.

Now lets' move on to Opportunity #2 – Ghostwriting

Chapter 3 – Opportunity #2: Ghostwriting

As described above, my book "Publish with a Purpose," describes the ghostwriting opportunity in detail.

Publish with a Purpose
http://www.amazon.com/dp/B008Z5U4LC

In this chapter I want to touch on some of the bullet points that make this a huge moneymaker. However; with that said, ghostwriting is not a passive income opportunity. You simply charge a fee to your customer who wants a book written but published under their own name as author.

Ghostwriting can be super profitable. Learn how to become a ghostwriter and how to write books for business owners at the same time. Once you purchase the "Publish with a Purpose" book, the download portal will also provide you with a sample video book trailer and sample legal agreement to use to contract your services with clients.

As a best-selling author, I command a high price for books that I ghostwrite. I charge anywhere from $997 to $5,000 per book with the average price being $2500 depending on the book, its content, length, etc. and it usually takes an average of about 30-days to complete

Who pays ghostwriters to ghostwrite books?

By far, the largest source of customers is business owners that use the books as business cards. Authors hold a certain amount of prestige amongst the general public and the service provider industry – lawyers, consultants, real estate agents and brokers, etc – are always contracting with me to ghostwrite their books. They use the books I write for them as justification that they are experts in their field and also use them as a kind of "business status symbol".

Once you begin ghostwriting, it quickly brings in customers by word-of mouth and you are not required to do any heavy advertising and or promotional work.

Here is a list of freelance sites where you can list your services and get job orders:

Freelance
http://www.agentsofvalue.com/
http://www.daydreamservices.com/
https://www.elance.com/
http://www.freelancer.com/
http://www.freelancers.net/
http://www.guru.com/
http://www.myzoox.com/
https://www.odesk.com/
http://www.peopleperhour.com/
http://www.skillwho.com/
http://workaholics4hire.com/

Once you have your book or a ghostwritten book published you will need to promote it. Here is a list of top promo sites:

Let These Sites Know 7+ Days Before Your Promo Starts
It's important to plan ahead your marketing for your free promotion. This list of sites requires 7+ days notice of your promo in order to post it.

http://www.pixelofink.com/sfkb/
http://bargainebookhunter.com/contact-us/
http://www.thatbookplace.com/free-promo-submissions/
http://indiebookoftheday.com/authors/free-on-kindle-listing/
http://www.freebookdude.com/p/list-your-free-book.html
http://the-cheap.net/authors/free-promotion-opportunities/share-your-deal/
http://awesomegang.com/submit-your-book/
http://www.fkbooksandtips.com/for-authors/
http://thefrugalereader.wufoo.com/forms/frugal-freebie-submissions/
http://ebookshabit.com/for-authors/
http://www.freebookshub.com/authors/
http://www.ebooksfreedaily.com/?page_id=16
http://ebooklister.net/submit.php
http://www.centsibleereads.com/p/for-authors.html
https://docs.google.com/spreadsheet/viewform?formkey=dHI3UVVZdTZkWUo3d2w3aDExbXk5MEE6MQ#gid=0
http://www.frugal-freebies.com/p/submit-freebie.html
http://onehundredfreebooks.com/contact.html
https://docs.google.com/spreadsheet/viewform?formkey=dFpBd0JUMk9KZzZ0TXJBYXRENFZYMVE6MQ

Fiction Sites
http://freekindlefiction.blogspot.com/p/tell-us-about-free-books.html
http://www.freebooksy.com/editorial-submissions
http://www.kindlemojo.com/contact-info/
http://www.centsibleereads.com/p/for-authors.html

Post On These Sites The Day Your Promo Starts Or 24 Hours Before
http://snickslist.com/books/place-ad/
http://www.freebookclub.org/kindle-books/book-submissions/
http://addictedtoebooks.com/free
http://www.daily-free-ebooks.com/suggest-free-ebook
http://www.ereaderiq.com/contact/

Free Book Twitter Influencers
These Twitter users all have medium to large followings on Twitter who love to hear about free books.

@freebookclub1
@ibdbookoftheday
@Booksontheknob
@bookbub
@kindle_free
@freeebooksdaily
@kindlefreebooks
@zilchebooks
@freedailybooks
@free2kindle
@freereadfeed
@pixelofink
@digitalinktoday
@fkbt
@kindlestuff
@free_kindle_fic
@Bookyrnextread
@CheapKindleDly
@DigitalBkToday
@kindlenews
@ebook
@freeebookdeal
@frcc
@free_kindle
@freebookdude
@4FreeKindleBook
@FreeKindleStuff
@IndAuthorSucess
@IndieKindle
@kindleebooks
@KindleBookKing
@KindleFreeBook
@KindleUpdates
@Kindle_promo
@KindleDaily
@WLCPromotions
UK Twitter Users:
@free_uk_ebooks

Facebook Groups For Authors

These are all great groups to join on Facebook to network and connect with other authors, share marketing ideas, ask questions and build relationships. I highly recommend you join these groups if you're a serious author!

https://www.facebook.com/groups/KindlePublishers/
https://www.facebook.com/groups/kindleauthors/
https://www.facebook.com/groups/357112331027292/
https://www.facebook.com/groups/bookmarketing/
https://www.facebook.com/groups/512098985483106/
https://www.facebook.com/groups/291645554239114/
https://www.facebook.com/groups/apablog/
https://www.facebook.com/groups/204725947524/
https://www.facebook.com/groups/204968026218845/
https://www.facebook.com/groups/2204546223/
https://www.facebook.com/groups/179494068820033/
https://www.facebook.com/groups/borntowrite/
https://www.facebook.com/groups/6092061939/
https://www.facebook.com/groups/135486133130440/
https://www.facebook.com/groups/110604178950149/

Facebook Groups For Fiction Authors

https://www.facebook.com/groups/fiction.nonfiction/
https://www.facebook.com/groups/174995555883415/
https://www.facebook.com/groups/2207480509/
https://www.facebook.com/groups/fanfictionlookout/

Facebook Groups For Promoting Your Free Books

https://www.facebook.com/groups/270558336379692/
https://www.facebook.com/groups/126278657527255/
https://www.facebook.com/groups/freebkrus/
https://www.facebook.com/groups/FreeTodayOnAmazon/
https://www.facebook.com/groups/215918835174776/
https://www.facebook.com/groups/1013820968756497/
https://www.facebook.com/groups/426282137432533/
https://www.facebook.com/groups/freeebooks/
https://www.facebook.com/groups/341840249197060/
https://www.facebook.com/groups/182637088529255/
https://www.facebook.com/groups/294455560643884/

https://www.facebook.com/groups/370900356880/
https://www.facebook.com/groups/236927589749427/

Personally, I am very heavily involved in book promotion and my free webinars explain some of the best techniques I use. But by far, invest in my following books to get the best understanding of how to sell books online and offline.

How to Promote Your Book Online & Offline
http://www.amazon.com/dp/B00AS7PDCK

How To Promote Your Book Online & Offline Vol 2
http://www.amazon.com/dp/B00BDTEILO

Promoting Your Video Book Trailers
http://www.amazon.com/dp/B00BCDHEMG

To date, I am responsible for thousands of people becoming authors and making big money online and they too enjoy the passive income while they continue to write and increase their book inventories.

Without a doubt, authorship and self-publishing offers the best passive income sources, ghostwriting can be accomplished in conjunction with an author's other activities.

You can become a ghostwriter or you can hire a ghostwriter to write your books. The majority of ghostwriters do not command my high fees because they are NOT best-selling authors. The average fee a ghostwriter charges for a 50-page book is $120. Most ebooks are 40-50 pages.

Okay, in the next chapter, I am going to teach you about "How to Become an Amateur Internet Sleuth," which is without a doubt the second best income source on the net today.

Chapter 4 - Opportunity #3: Amateur Internet Sleuth

Think about it; cyber crime is going out of sight as the economy worsens. Here is an article from the New York Times to demonstrate just how weird things are getting...

Editorial
Sneaky Apps That Track Cellphones
Published: December 23, 2012

http://www.nytimes.com/2012/12/24/opinion/sneaking-after-cellphone-users.html?nl=todaysheadlines&emc=edit_th_20121224&_r=0

A perversion of smartphone technology called "stalking apps" — precise, secretive tracking of the movements of cellphone users — is increasingly a matter of national concern, particularly for domestic abuse victims. No less threatening is the routine monitoring of children's locales and phone habits for commercial purposes while parents are kept in the dark. Stealth apps even stoop to cyber-leering through the now notorious app called Girls Around Me, which allows men to search out women, unbeknown to them, by cross-matching GPS technology with information and photo sites like Facebook.

With these abuses proliferating, the Senate Judiciary Committee this month took a big step to protect the privacy of all cellphone users and close legal loopholes that enable stalking apps. The committee approved a worthy measure sponsored by Senator Al Franken, Democrat of Minnesota that for the first time would require cellphone companies to obtain a user's permission to collect location data and sell it or share it with third parties. It also would flatly outlaw creation of stalking apps, applying criminal and civil penalties.

"Right now companies — some legitimate, some sleazy — are collecting yoursw or your child's location and selling it to ad companies or who knows who else," Mr. Franken told the committee. He described a constituent who was not aware that her spouse had secretly installed an app on her phone to stalk her movements — and send her text threats along the way — as she went to court for a protection order. It takes mere seconds, the senator said, for an abuser to slip a stalking app into another person's phone. The need to protect children was echoed in a recent Federal Trade Commission study showing that some of the most popular apps for children engage in commercial phone stalking, with no notification to parents.

Current laws banning stalking and wiretapping lag behind modern communications, with no provision barring companies from marketing a stalking app. One company sells such an app for about $50, and advertised on its site: "Suspect your spouse is cheating? Don't break the bank by hiring a private investigator."

The measure is opposed by software companies, which say they can police themselves. This is highly unlikely considering the money to be made by this lucrative and fast-moving technology. The Senate should approve the measure and move it for House action with speed worthy of the Internet.

*****

I am very big in forensic science and privacy issues because I see the damage being done daily to companies and people from hackers and crackers. As big as my ForensicsNation unit is – 22,000 cyber forensics investigators in 22-counties, WE DON'T EVEN MAKE A DENT in cyber-crime. I write the software that catches to bad guys online. Cyber-criminals have no idea how we track them down and nab the.

What I have put together form y readers is a program where it teaches you to track down cyber-criminals and turn them in to law enforcement and collect the reward. It is called the ForensicsNation Bushwhacker Program.

FNC Bushwhacker Program
http://www.amazon.com/dp/B007I9AHVS

Everything in this program is done from home. You never see or confront the cyber-criminal. There are hundreds of 'wanted' websites on the net that list the cyber-criminal and the reward. Using the program outlined above, you can easily find and track cyber-criminals. If they own a cellphone, laptop, tablet and are online YOU OWN THEM.

The FNC Bushwhacker Program also teaches you how to protect you and your loved ones too.

Let me give you an example of ways to make money. I charge $497 to scan a cell phone for spyware planted on it and remove it if found. Ex-wife, ex-husbands and tons of other perpetrators are constantly planting spyware on cell phones for nefarious reasons. In any given week I scan and clean 25-30 cellphones. Do the math!!

Here is another moneymaker. I offer a service that scans a residence or business for hidden cameras and listening devices. I charge $497 for this service. With the new wireless technology, cameras are as small as a button and can transmit what it see wirelessly over the internet. I get more requests for services form college students than any other customer and I usually find hidden cameras spying on them too. Flipping weird!!!!

I had one customer – she was a waitress for the restaurant chain Hooters – call me and when I scanned outside her bedroom window, I found a wireless camera in a tree and it was in the process of transmitting so I track the signal down the street to find a guy in a car with a handheld viewing device. You should have seen his face when the cops surrounded his car and yanked him out of the vehicle. He is now serving five years for voyeurism.

People, it never ends. There is so much business out there you simply can't get to all of it or train personnel to handle it.

The opportunities are endless in the forensics business. As a forensics investigator your job is to track the dirtbag down, compile and preserve the evidence. YOU ARE NOT A PEACE OFFICER and you do not have arresting authority so you never confront the dirtbag; you call in law enforcement to do the bust.

You are not a private investigator and you do no field work whatsoever. The services I cited above are not investigative field work. You are not tracking anybody; you are simply providing a service. Hence you do not need any special licensing.

When you become an amateur internet sleuth – bushwhacker- you will find an interesting thing that develops. You begin to "specialize" in certain internet crime. I have bushwhackers that specialize in identity theft, spyware, cyber stalkers, and more. I, myself, specialize in child predators and child abusers because it is one of my passions as you can tell from the books I write on the subject and more:

Confessions of a Child Predator
http://www.amazon.com/dp/B007BB97KU

Child Watch
http://www.amazon.com/dp/B0095K1P3M

Cyber-Daters Beware
http://www.amazon.com/dp/B006J9T4NA

Cyber Protect Your Business
http://www.amazon.com/dp/B0095JEAYY

ForensicsNation Bushwhacker Program
http://www.amazon.com/dp/B007I9AHVS

ForensicsNationsStore.com Catalog
http://ForensicsNationStore.com

Protecting Yourself from Cyber Crime
http://www.amazon.com/dp/B0095J3EIW

Stealing You
http://www.amazon.com/dp/B00778TT6E

Was Sandy Hook a Hoax?
http://www.amazon.com/dp/B00BFSM8IS

Why Women Should Not Use Online Dating Services
http://www.amazon.com/dp/B006J9EMH8

You Can Run But You Cannot Hide
http://www.amazon.com/dp/B006JLVZC6

Yes, you can become a bushwhacker and couple this with your authorship and make money in multiple income streams.

Are you smelling what we are stepping in here, people? All of the above that I taught you so far is accomplished from your home.

Your home is the central core of your existence. You first become lean and mean and then turn your home into **passive and active income sources** by following the bouncing ball of the things I am teaching you.

The operative word here is HOME! By working from your home, you have more time to spend with your kids and family and think of the money you will save in day care.

By working from home you literally cut down on expenses – dry cleaning, wear and tear on your car, fuel bills, and more.

The benefits far outpace the negatives. Now let's talk about Opportunity #4 – Survival Planning…

Chapter 5 – Opportunity #4: Survival Planning

I am very big on this subject and I make no qualms about it. The operative word here is PLANNING. My corporate motto is "Be prepared to Survive!"

I have written extensively on this subject with most of my books skyrocketing to best-selling status within just a few days:

Be A Prepper
http://www.amazon.com/dp/B007IL5OE6

PrepperNations Blueprint
http://www.amazon.com/dp/B00ARBZNCW

Be Prepared to Survive
http://www.amazon.com/dp/B007KJ0ANQ

SurvivalNations Catalog
http://www.barnesandnoble.com/w/survivalnations-catalog-dr-leland-benton/1037736612?ean=2940013745148&itm=2&usri=dr.+leland+benton

SurvivalNations - Surviving a Disease Pandemic
http://www.amazon.com/dp/B00BFFZCHU

Surviving A Financial Crisis
http://www.amazon.com/dp/B007J1QH3C

Surviving YOU
http://www.amazon.com/dp/B007J3M6A8

The Truth About Federal Anti-Hoarding Laws
http://www.amazon.com/dp/B007J4KH4O

Let me tell you how I got into this segment of business. I was in Las Vegas shopping with my girlfriend at the Fashion Show Mall. She was trying on clothes and doing what women do when shopping when suddenly she came running out to tell me she thought the changing room mirror was a two-way mirror. I had taught her how to check the mirrors to see if they were two-way so I went in and verified, yes it was a two-way mirror. I went up to the sales clerk and asked her to call thee manager. When the manager arrived, I demonstrated that his store had two-way mirrors in the dressing rooms. He informed me and my girlfriend that it was necessary to cut down on shoplifting. I informed him that it was illegal to have two-way mirrors in the dressing rooms even if he posted it on the outside of each dressing room, which it wasn't.

I then called the police and filed a report for voyeurism. Next I filed a lawsuit against the store, which was quickly settled out of court. My girlfriend and I returned to this store months later and the two-way mirrors had been removed. This is why survival planning and privacy issues are both big topics with me.

In my book PrepperNations Blueprint, I describe how I began forming neighborhood survival groups and providing my neighbors with survival products.

PrepperNations Blueprint
http://www.amazon.com/dp/B00ARBZNCW

This wasn't about selling products; the selling part was the effect; the cause was providing a needed service to my community. The concept literally took off with people emailing me how to duplicate what I was doing in their neighborhoods nationwide. All of this activity came from publishing my book PrepperNations Blueprint.

From this one book I wrote a survival checklist book called "Be Prepared to Survive" and it offered a complete checklist of what to consider in survival planning so nothing was left out. Along with this book I published a survival catalog of products that I personally use and could vouch for call SurvivalNations catalog.

Be Prepared to Survive
http://www.amazon.com/dp/B007KJ0ANQ

SurvivalNations Catalog
http://www.barnesandnoble.com/w/survivalnations-catalog-dr-leland-benton/1037736612?ean=2940013745148&itm=2&usri=dr.+leland+benton

Just last week from writing this I published "SurvivalNations - Surviving a Disease Pandemic," which also skyrocketed to best-selling status in just a few days.

SurvivalNations - Surviving a Disease Pandemic
http://www.amazon.com/dp/B00BFFZCHU

My point is this: this is a topic that is on a good many people's minds. Think about it, the evening news is full of natural disasters from hurricanes to tsunamis, earthquakes to volcanic eruptions. And if Mother Nature isn't enough, the evening news is full of the assault on our schools and children, mass murders, child predators, white slavery, and more. Everywhere we turn some disaster and or crisis is rearing its ugly head.

Then we have government that can't get their act together. There is no bi-partisanship, no agreement on anything. The 2012 elections were a joke; the fact that the country is broke doesn't seem to bother anybody as government spending continues to spin out of control.

And then you have the European union coming apart at the seams. There is rioting in Greece and Spain over austerity measures. Italy is just about ready to blow up and more.

Last but not least, you have the results of the Arab spring uprisings in 2012 with Egypt, Tunisia, Libya and now Syria throwing off the dictator yokes and replacing them with what? More dictators? Yep!

With all of what I said above, is survival planning necessary? You betcha! And what is the central core of your existence…your HOME!

Now let's talk about Opportunity #5: Internet Marketing…

Chapter 6 – Opportunity #5: Internet Marketing

I have been an Internet marketer since the net became public in 1989. Back then we only had email marketing to sell our stuff. Times have sure changed.

I am not going to get into everything that Internet marketing involves, otherwise this book would be the size of "War and Peace".

In Internet marketing there are two systems that dominate. They are affiliate marketing and cost-per-action marketing or CPA marketing. Both of these programs are where you sell other people's products. I don't do these; I don't sell products I have no control over.

I sell my products because I can control the quality, the quantity, the customer service and the fulfillment. Not because I am a control freak – I am – but because I have a saying I have used to guide me in business for quite a long time – **"A sale does not stop at the exchange of legal tender; it has only just begun."**

The most important part of a sale is customer service. My words mean nothing unless people put them into practice and since everybody is different when it comes to learning, I want to make myself available if they get stuck so they do it right the first time. In all of my books I give my personal email address and I really do respond to each one.

So, in this book I want to concentrate on Internet marketing where you are selling YOUR products and not other people's products.

Okay, in the book "Getting Paid For Everything You Do," it provides literally oodles of resources of tasks for a person to do and get paid for their daily work. It rocks and I have already said that this book should be in your personal library.

This book is for people that do not have a high skill level using a computer or have some difficulty learning new things. Unfortunately this is not my book but like I said, I was the adviser on the book and I know it inside and out so if you buy it and get stuck, write to me if you need help.

This book is perfect for senior citizens who did not grow up in the computer age and cannot find work because of their age.

Getting Paid For EVERYTHING You Do!
http://www.amazon.com/dp/B00B03C0EA

I will tell you a little story to demonstrate how serious I am to customer service. A lady – Lori S - bought one of my books and wrote to me that she was having trouble implementing the programs. She lived in Los Angeles, which is about 6.5 hours from where I live. After numerous emails, I called her and she told me that she had four kids and her husband was laid off from his job. She was desperate to find income and had bought my book to do it. It turned out she had very little computer skills – could barely turn the computer on – and this was the reason for her problem.

Well, I grew up in Los Angeles – I am also a UCLA alumnus – so I decided to go pay Lori and her husband a visit and see how the old neighborhoods looked. WOW- did Los Angeles ever change but that is a good subject for another book. I have to tell you, the look on both of Lori and her husband's faces when I showed up armed with my laptop and air card was priceless. They simply could not believe that I would take my time and drive out to Los Angeles to help them.

Anyway, helping them was not easy because they both were practically brain dead using a computer so what I did was write out a simple tutorial on Step 1 then Step 2, etc and Lori was not to move on to the next step until she had mastered the first step, etc. this technique actually solved the problem because it forced Lori to concentrate step-by-step until she completed a task and got paid.

The reason why I bring up Lori and her husband is that I spoke to both of them just last week. She is up to $3,000/month and is no longer on food stamps or unemployment insurance. Her husband has quit looking for a job and is helping her with her new online business. He even enrolled in the local city college for computer science courses and loving it.

It was nice helping them but I did get a chance to visit all of my old neighborhoods and stomping grounds. I simply cannot believe how the place had changed so dramatically. Santa Monica is now yuppie land with street markets and tons of tiny little bistros and coffee houses. I even got a chance to go to the beach and soak up some rays…that was really nice.

I stopped by all of the neighborhoods I lived in and came across one of the houses I lived in in 1966. It was for sale so I called the realtor listed on the sign. My dad paid $38,500 for this house in 1966 and the sale price was now $750,000. OMG – I am convinced that everybody in California is smoking crack cocaine. How do young people begin their lives with real estate prices like that? Bloody, flipping amazing; but that is not all.

My family moved to California from New York in 1954. We first lived in San Diego but there were no jobs so we moved to Los Angeles and lived in Venice on the canals. Venice Canals was an attempt by a local developer to replicate the ones in Italy but was a dismal failure. Back then the canals were filthy and stagnant.

Anyway, I went back to see if the canals were still there and they were. The house I lived in was still there too but had been heavily updated and remodeled. It wasn't for sale but the one next door was so I called the realtor. Are you sitting down? The list price on the house was $2.2 million dollars. My dad paid $16,500 for the house next door in 1954. Is it any wonder why people are fleeing out of California? Even if I didn't own a car, I would walk out of that state just to get away from it...sheesh! Oh, and I almost forgot; the canals were still filthy and stagnant...amazing!

Okay enough of walking down memory lane...

Like I said, Internet marketing involves many aspects. To demonstrate, here is a list of my books just on Internet Marketing and Mobile Commerce, which is a sub-division of Internet marketing.

21st Century Marketing Genius
http://www.amazon.com/dp/B008A07WBW

AWeber For Dummies
http://www.amazon.com/dp/B006IVMP8A

BlueprintCashPro
http://www.amazon.com/dp/B006X0UASS

CashCodePro
http://www.amazon.com/dp/B006WZRCVM

Distraction Marketing
http://www.amazon.com/dp/B006IUVBWM

Effective Email Advertising
http://www.amazon.com/dp/B006IV2300

Fast TV EXPOSURE
http://www.amazon.com/dp/B00939A1YY

In-Image Ads Marketing
http://www.amazon.com/dp/B006X03NBE

Massive Traffic Generator
http://www.amazon.com/dp/B006IV1YRS

Pay Per Call Marketing
http://www.amazon.com/dp/B006XVUD98

Pay Per View Advertising
http://www.amazon.com/dp/B006ZXMI4W

PLR Cash Tactics
http://www.amazon.com/dp/B006IVGBDU

SEONemo ThenSEO
http://www.amazon.com/dp/B006JN54LW

SEONemo NowSEO
http://www.amazon.com/dp/B006JMYHYI

SEONemo SoonSEO
http://www.amazon.com/dp/B006JN5606

Social Media Marketing
http://www.amazon.com/dp/B006Z7VSGW

The Perfect Affiliate
http://www.amazon.com/dp/B007RN2T5M

The Postcarders
http://www.amazon.com/dp/B006IUUV6O

Traffic Jam
http://www.amazon.com/dp/B007SXI0YK

Traffic Media
http://www.amazon.com/dp/B006IUZV28

Video Marketing
http://www.amazon.com/dp/B006XW0J0U

Web Traffic Systems
http://www.amazon.com/dp/B006IVGYAA

Word of Mouth Marketing (WOMM)
http://www.amazon.com/dp/B006X0FXU8

Mobile Commerce

It's All About Database
http://www.amazon.com/dp/B006JO0RBI

Mobile Commerce Blueprint
http://www.amazon.com/dp/B006JO1CX0

Mobile Text Voting
http://www.amazon.com/dp/B006JOI4ZO

Selling Air
http://www.amazon.com/dp/B006JOIS5K

SMS Mobile Competitions
http://www.amazon.com/dp/B006JO1MLC

SMS Reverse Auction
http://www.amazon.com/dp/B006JOYKI4

To Boldly Go Mobile
http://www.amazon.com/dp/B006JNJTEK

As you can see, Internet Marketing is nothing to sneeze at and involves many different aspects.

Out of all of the above I want to specifically talk about one really neat one called The Postcarders:

The Postcarders
http://www.amazon.com/dp/B006IUUV6O

This is an automated postcard marketing program where you can sell your products using postcards BUT, everything is fully automated and you accomplish all of your marketing campaigns from your computer. You never touch or see the postcard. You design the postcard and offer on your computer. Then you provide a mailing list and the websites stated in the book will print the postcard, address the postcard, stamp it and mail it for you. Like I said, you never see or touch the postcard.

I love this program and to date I send out about 250,000 postcards each month. One thing I learned; there are people that refuse to use a computer. They don't own one; they do not have an email address…nothing. These are my best customers because they respond well to my offers.

Here is another very weird thing that a gentleman I spoke to at a convention one day years ago taught me and it was a hard lesson to learn too. It is so weird; I am even having trouble putting it into words.

Here is a postcard I designed for one of my products:

It was four colors on gloss enamel paper and did okay sales-wise until I showed it to the gentleman in question. BTW – this gentleman was labeled the "Postcard King" at the convention. He took one look at it and said I did it all wrong. He said it was too pretty and I needed to make it ugly. Then it would sell like hotcakes. To prove his point, he whipped out his laptop and said this is the postcard I should send:

How to overcome financial meltdown

Has someone stolen your time, talents and energy in return for some low paying wage or salary?

Has someone stolen your peace and well-being as you stress over your current financial condition?

Has Someone Stolen YOU?

We can help!

Candidly, I took one look at what he presented and then looked at him and said, "You have got to be kidding me!!!" And he wasn't; he told me to go and run the same campaign as I did with the pretty one substituting the ugly one and see the results for myself.

Reluctantly and I mean reluctantly, I did what he suggested and then almost fell over when the results came in. The ugly card out sold the pretty card like 5-to1. Bloody, flipping amazing! Don't even ask me why because I still, to this day, can't figure it out but the facts speak for themselves; when it comes to postcard marketing, ugly is better than pretty. That should be a bumper sticker!!!

Okay, in the next chapter I am going to list various opportunities available that you can easily implement. These opportunities I canister to be less meatier than the ones I have presented so far so study each one carefully to see if you have a passion for it.

Chapter 7 – Opportunity #6: Miscellaneous Opportunities

1. Advice & How To: If you select writing books then the genre called Advice & How To without a doubt is the most lucrative genre and this is where I make the most money. To wit: here is a list of my books in this genre:

 Advice/How To

Applied Mind Sciences
http://www.amazon.com/dp/B007GK4U08

Addictions
http://www.amazon.com/dp/B006IGHQD4

Anatomy of Anxiety
http://www.amazon.com/dp/B00777QQYS

A Weapon of Massive Consumption
http://www.amazon.com/dp/B008SUWGZG

A Woman Surrounds A Man
http://www.amazon.com/dp/B008DY2VDO

Blame Me Not

http://www.amazon.com/dp/B008D37AI6

Body Language
http://www.amazon.com/dp/B006INI18G

Body Talk
http://www.amazon.com/dp/B0079MA1XS

Bouncing Back From Adversity to Success
http://www.amazon.com/dp/B008ZSGPRQ

Bully America
http://www.amazon.com/dp/B008EJ6102

Cartoon Psychology
http://www.amazon.com/dp/B006IUHMN4

Chasing Shadows
http://www.amazon.com/dp/B008A5ZRW8

Confessions of a Child Predator
http://www.amazon.com/dp/B007BB97KU

Confessions of a Satanic Worshipper
http://www.amazon.com/dp//B007DR4838

Control Your Dreams
http://www.amazon.com/dp/B0071YN3L6

Fantasy Is Easy-Everything Is Perfect
http://www.amazon.com/dp/B00BFF81CS

Female Wolf Packs
http://www.amazon.com/dp/B006JMHD80

Gender Differences in Advertising
http://www.amazon.com/dp/B006IOCG9U

How Do I Let Go?

http://www.amazon.com/dp/B00AW18EFK

How To Cope with Male Menopause
http://www.amazon.com/dp/B00ATLAEVA

If It Is Broke; Fix It
http://www.amazon.com/dp/B006JM6NHM

I Have a Mind to Believe
http://www.amazon.com/dp/B006ITGY84

I Know I Am But Who Are You
http://www.amazon.com/dp/B006IOQL7I

Interesting Facts About Left-Handed People
http://www.amazon.com/dp/B00744PXCA

Living Alone
http://www.amazon.com/dp/B0086O1ZC4

Love is the Way
http://www.amazon.com/dp/B006IVYPFG

Male-Female Realities
http://www.amazon.com/dp/B006ITYUNK

Man Up - The Decline and Fall of Manhood
http://www.amazon.com/dp/B006JA2UMG

Men & Women…attract or attack
http://www.amazon.com/dp/B006IU8LU2

Predictable Advertising
http://www.amazon.com/dp/B00B0SWNPG

Questions
http://www.amazon.com/dp/B006WQ715S

Satisfaction

http://www.amazon.com/dp/B006JM6ING

Sexting & Text Flirting
http://www.barnesandnoble.com/w/sexting-text-flirting-noah-pranksky/1108217620?ean=2940013770348&itm=1&usri=sexting+%26+text+flirting

Teen Idols
http://www.amazon.com/dp/B006IWNPYC

The Color of White
http://www.amazon.com/dp/B008GNIOTM

The Denial of Self
http://www.amazon.com/dp/B008B7OK32

The Face of Anorexia
http://www.amazon.com/dp/B007F8M4XG

The Face Of Despair
http://www.amazon.com/dp/B006JPOV2S

The Greatest Fraud the World Has Ever Known
http://www.amazon.com/dp/B008GUBKI2

The Missing Link
http://www.amazon.com/dp/B006WQLNTI

The Other Side of Me
http://www.amazon.com/dp/B006JMYAE0

The Power of Concentration
http://www.barnesandnoble.com/w/the-power-of-concentration-dr-harry-jay/1114037587?ean=2940016133140

The Power of Observation
http://www.amazon.com/dp/B006IU99EY

The Science of Psychology EXPOSED

http://www.amazon.com/dp/B007JBR682

The Smack Report
http://www.amazon.com/dp/B007AZIELK

The Vowel Movement
http://www.amazon.com/dp/B0071NUPZY

Too Late For Fruit; Too Soon For Flowers
http://www.amazon.com/dp/B006IVLXSI

What Is It About Yorkies
http://www.amazon.com/dp/B006JMNRQW

Will I Look Good In This
http://www.amazon.com/dp/B007NCFZ30

Wordz
http://www.amazon.com/dp/B006IOCSVQ

You Can't or You Won't
http://www.amazon.com/dp/B007FQ2EJ2

I have published a list of Amazon categories that demonstrate just how many genres and categories are available for you to write about. I couldn't include it in this book because it is 138-pages. Go here and download it for free:

http://tinyurl.com/epubwebinar2

If this doesn't get your creative juice flowing nothing will!

2. Health & Fitness: Another genre that is super lucrative is health and fitness. It is my second most profitable niche. To wit: here are some of the books I have published:

Health/Fitness/Alternative Medicine

Chelation Therapy

http://www.amazon.com/dp/B006J7YZ54

Drop Three Dress Sizes in 30-Days
http://www.amazon.com/dp/B007F7VHZI

Embarrassing Problems Fix - General Problems Vol 1
http://www.amazon.com/dp/B0075LOK3U

Embarrassing Problems Fix - Female Problems Vol 2
http://www.amazon.com/dp/B0075LO7AQ

Embarrassing Problems Fix - Male Problems Vol 3
http://www.amazon.com/dp/B0075LQNF8

Energy Psychology
http://www.amazon.com/dp/B006JOZ7G8

Getting Rid of Cellulite in 10-Days
http://www.amazon.com/dp/B008XB1A34

If You Want to Get Big Eat a Pig
http://www.amazon.com/dp/B00AYCX5PQ

PhattyFat WheytLoss
http://www.amazon.com/dp/B00779O2JW

The Complete Health System
http://www.amazon.com/dp/B006IVHG2K

The Pain Game
http://www.amazon.com/dp/B007DIPZX4

The Way to Flat Abs in 4-Weeks
http://www.barnesandnoble.com/w/the-way-to-flat-abs-in-4-weeks-noah-pransky/1108217624?ean=2940013770416&itm=1&usri=the+way+to+flat+abs+in+4+weeks

NOTE: if you write in multiple genres then use a pen name for each genre so as not to confuse your readers.

3. Investment/Income: Still another very lucrative genre is investment/income and this is my third most profitable niche.

Investment/Income

Applied Income Model
http://www.amazon.com/dp/B006WZN8M4
http://www.barnesandnoble.com/w/applied-income-model-dr-leland-benton/1108229415?ean=2940013744950

Getting Paid For EVERYTHING You Do!
http://www.amazon.com/dp/B00B03C0EA

How to Choose a Good Trading System
http://www.amazon.com/dp/B00B0ONI4K

How To Marry Into Wealth
http://www.barnesandnoble.com/w/how-to-marry-into-wealth-noah-pranksky/1108197735?ean=2940013753297&itm=1&usri=how+to+marry+into+wealth

How To Monetize Social Trends
http://www.barnesandnoble.com/w/how-to-monetize-social-media-trends-noah-pranksky/1108217569?ean=2940013770300&itm=1&usri=how+to+monetize+social+media+trends

How To Retire Without Money
http://www.amazon.com/dp/B00B5R2ORE

Money Is an Effect and Not a Cause
http://www.amazon.com/dp/B008ZGM2MK

The Psychology of Sales
http://www.amazon.com/dp/B006IUH0GI

Triggers That Cause Buyers to Open Their Wallets
http://www.amazon.com/dp/B00ASWOT7K

4. DIY – Do it Yourself: There is one more very profitable niche that really rocks but I do not write in this niche because I am the most un-mechanical person on the planet. UL Laboratories could hire me to figure out how to break a product. If it's breakable you can bet I will find a way to do it. I am literally all thumbs when it comes to even the most simple mechanical; tasks. But just because I am a "lamer' when it comes to DIY doesn't means you are. This is a very lucrative niche and if you have a passion for doing anything with your hands then this is the niche for you.

When I buy Kindle books online – and I buy a ton of them – I usually buy books from the DIY niche. The lat book I bought was on woodworking and although I suck at woodworking I am determined to learn it. Thankfully I can do this in the privacy of my own home because if you were to watch me, you would probably end up soiling yourself with laughter…yeah I am that bad at it.

Thankfully, I have a brother-in-law that is very mechanical and he helps me around the hose. He knows I am partially retarded when it comes to anything mechanical and is patient with me. Also my garage is the paradise of tools. Amazing, eh? Here I am the most un-mechanical person on the planet yet I have every tool under the sun…and this was even after I downsized!!! My brother-in-law told my sister that I have more stuff in my garage then the local Ace Hardware Store and he isn't kidding.

I even have one of those four-wheel ATVs with a little trailer that I can pull behind it. I also bought the snow plow attachment and I really use this baby a lot. Where I live we get a lot of snow.

The ATV is also fun to take out into the woods. My Yorkie, Gage and I go whenever we get the opportunity and campout. I had a harrowing experience happen to me on one such campout. I built a little wire basket on the back of the ATV to hold my Yorkie and some camping stuff when we go out. On one excursion, Gage was barking up a storm and I turned to look at what he was barking at just in time to wave off a big red tail hawk that had his eye on making Gage his dinner. That scared me so I built a lid on the basket and keep a sharp eye out when Gage is with me. He doesn't go more than a couple of feet from me when we are in the woods.

4. Email Marketing: I began in the business, like I said previously, using Email Marketing as my primary marketing system mainly because in 1989 this is all we had. But email marketing has evolved into a very lucrative business model if done correctly. I simply cannot go into this marketing system in detail; there is too much to teach you. I wrote four books on the subject that teaches it to you step-by-step:

21st Century Marketing Genius
http://www.amazon.com/dp/B008A07WBW

AWeber For Dummies
http://www.amazon.com/dp/B006IVMP8A

Effective Email Advertising
http://www.amazon.com/dp/B006IV2300

Distraction Marketing
http://www.amazon.com/dp/B006IUVBWM

Here is an inside tip: My "Distraction Marketing" book describes an email marketing technique that makes me gobs of money and when you read it you will see why. But first order the "Effective Email Advertising" book since it is the bible of email marketing. Once you learn email marketing then read the "Distraction Marketing" book.

Chapter 8 – Summary & Conclusions

Now I want to summarize everything I have taught you. In the introduction to this book I wanted you to learn that to gain you must lose and to lose you must gain. Life is a divine balance so every time you suffer a loss then look for the gain. I also wanted to introduce to you some great books that would provide you with daily moneymaking opportunities and were both a good starting point for people with limited computer skills

In Chapter 1, my goal was to teach you to downsize and get rid of stuff you simply do not use and get rid of the expense of storing it too. You will be amazed at how exhilarating it is to be rid of the responsibility of it not to mention the expense.

In Chapter 2 and subsequent chapters, my goal was to begin offering the meatier 'career' type opportunities for people really wanting to get serious working from home. I first taught you to look at the asset and income side of your personal budget and downsize the asset side while upsizing the income side using passive income techniques. The best passive income technique is book writing and publishing and I used this technique because it is something everybody can do.

In Chapter 3, I introduced you to ghostwriting and taught you how to make money as a ghostwriter. Although this is not a passive moneymaking technique it is still quite lucrative and is an option to consider.

In Chapter 4, I introduced you to the amateur Internet sleuth opportunity call the FNC Bushwhacker program. I gave you some different examples of techniques to specialize in and how to get started.

The next lucrative opportunity was survival planning and how I do it. I emphasized the importance of doing things you have a passion for at the same time showing you what works for me and niches I am involved in that are the most lucrative. Your passions may be different and that is okay but be sure to research each niche you may be considering to see if it is lucrative.

In Chapter 6, I described some Internet marketing opportunities and although I do have fun in this niche I have listed the ones I love the most in the order I really enjoy them. This niche is not for everybody and I stressed the importance of marketing your own products rather than other people's products.

Last, in Chapter 7, I listed some lucrative miscellaneous opportunities and again, let your passions be your guide. I wanted to make you aware of the various opportunities available to you and that you are not stuck with everyday stuff that everybody is doing.

I want to thank my readers for their patronage. Now I have a special gift for you. Please read on...

I Have a Special Gift for My Readers

I appreciate my readers for without them I am just another author attempting to make a difference. If my book has made a favorable impression please leave me an honest review. Thank you in advance for you participation.

My readers and I have in common a passion for the written word as well as the desire to learn and grow from books.

My special offer to you is a massive ebook library that I have compiled over the years. It contains hundreds of fiction and non-fiction ebooks in Adobe Acrobat PDF format as well as the Greek classics and old literary classics too.

In fact, this library is so massive to completely download the entire library will require over 5 GBs open on your desktop.

Use the link below and scan all of the ebooks in the library. You can select the ebooks you want individually or download the entire library.

The link below does not expire after a given time period so you are free to return for more books rather than clog your desktop. And feel free to give the link to your friends who enjoy reading too.

I thank you for reading my book and hope if you are pleased that you will leave me an honest review so that I can improve my work and or write books that appeal to your interests.

Okay, here is the link…

http://tinyurl.com/special-readers-promo

PS: If you wish to reach me personally for any reason you may simply write to mailto:support@epubwealth.com.

I answer all of my emails so rest assured I will respond.

Meet the Author
Dr. Leland Benton is Director of Applied Web Info, a holding company for ePubWealth.com, a leading ePublisher company based in Utah. With over 21,000 resellers in over 22-countries, ePubWealth.com is a leader in ePublishing, book promotion, and ebook marketing.

As the creator and author of "The ePubWealth Program," Leland teaches up-and-coming authors the ins-and-outs of today's ePublishing world. He has assisted hundreds of authors make it big in the ePublishing world.

Leland also created a series of external book promotion programs and teaches authors how to promote their books using external marketing sources.

Leland is also the Managing Director of Applied Mind Sciences, the company's mind research unit and Chief Forensics Investigator for the company's ForensicsNation unit. He is active in privacy rights through the company's PrivacyNations unit and is an expert in survival planning and disaster relief through the company's SurvivalNations unit.

Leland resides in Southern Utah.

http://www.amazon.com/author/lelandbenton

www.ingramcontent.com/pod-product-compliance
Lightning Source LLC
Chambersburg PA
CBHW071640170526
45166CB00003B/1376